THE TRUTH IS

1. Leveling up your craft to write a story that lives long after you've left the planet is what some might call a ridiculous goal.

2. You know that you will not tell that story after reading just one how-to-write book.

3. You know that you will not tell that story as the result of taking one seminar.

4. You know that creating a timeless work of art will require the dedication of a world-class athlete. You will be training your mind with as much ferocity and single-minded purpose as an Olympic gold medal hopeful. That kind of cognitive regimen excites you, but you just haven't found a convincing storytelling dojo to do that work.

5. The path to leveling up your creative craft is a dark and treacherous course. You've been at it a long time, and it often feels like you're wearing three-dimensional horse blinders. More times than you'd wish to admit, you're not sure if you are moving north or south or east or west. And the worst part? You can't see anyone else, anywhere going through what you're going through. You're all alone.

WELCOME TO THE STORY GRID UNIVERSE. HERE'S HOW WE CONTEND WITH THOSE TRUTHS:

1. We believe we find meaning in the pursuit of creations that last longer than we do. It is not ridiculous. Dedicating our work to seizing opportunities and overcoming obstacles as we stretch ourselves to reach for seemingly unreachable creations is transformational. We believe this pursuit is the most valuable and honorable way to spend our time here. Even if...especially if...we never reach our lofty creative goals.

2. Writing just one story isn't going to take us to the top. We're moving from point A to Point A^{5000}. We've got lots of mountains to climb, lots of rivers and oceans to cross, and many deep dark forests to traverse in our way. We need topographic guides on demand, and if they're not available now, we'll have to figure it out and write them ourselves.

3. While we're drawn to seminars to consume the imparted wisdom from an icon in the arena, we leave with something far more valuable than the curriculum. We get to meet the universe's other pilgrims and compare notes on the terrain.

4. The Story Grid Universe has a virtual dojo, a university to work out and get stronger—the place to stumble, correct the mistakes, and stumble again until the moves become automatic, lethal, and mesmerizing to outside observers.

5. The Story Grid Universe has a performance space, a publishing house dedicated to leveling up the craft with clear boundaries of progress, and the ancillary reference resources to pack for each project mission. There is an infinite number of paths to where you want to be with a story that works. Seeing how others made it down their own private yellow brick roads to release their creations into the timeless creative cosmos will help keep you on the straight and narrow path.

All are welcome—the more, the merrier—but please abide by the golden rule.

Put the Work Above All Else, and trust the process.

WHAT'S THE BIG IDEA?

NONFICTION CONDENSED

LESLIE WATTS
SHELLEY SPERRY

STORY GRID

STORY GRID

Story Grid Publishing LLC
223 Egremont Plain Road
PMB 191
Egremont, MA 01230

Copyright (c) 2020 Story Grid Publishing LLC
Cover Design by Magnus Rex
Edited by Shawn Coyne

All Rights Reserved

First Story Grid Publishing Paperback Edition March 2020

For Information about Special Discounts for Bulk Purchases,

Please visit www.storygridpublishing.com

ISBN: 978-1-64501-042-5
Ebook: 978-1-64501-043-2

For

All Past, Present, and Future Story Nerds

INTRODUCTION

"Writing is learned by imitation. If anyone asked me how I learned to write, I'd say I learned by reading the men and women who were doing the kind of writing I wanted to do and trying to figure out how they did it."

—William Zinsser, *On Writing Well*[1]

You've picked up this book because you have an exciting idea about a phenomenon or problem in the world. You think your idea will help other people understand the phenomenon or even solve the problem. You've already studied it and done some research. Maybe you've also written an article or some blog posts about it. But you realize that the next step in reaching the people who need to know about your idea is pretty daunting. You need to write a book.

And you probably need to write what we call a Big Idea book—one that takes apart a phenomenon or problem, looks at it through several lenses, and brings readers new insights and ways of putting those insights into practice.

Undertaking any big project, but especially a book, is a daunting proposition. The way to make it less scary is to have a map for the journey, and ideally, some experienced fellow travelers to ride shotgun—friends who know the road well and can help you make it to your destination. That's what we are aiming to provide.

We're two editors with over twenty years of experience between us, writing and editing many types of nonfiction. In the pages that follow, we distill some of the lessons we've learned in the trenches applying Shawn Coyne's Story Grid methodology to the work of our clients, all of whom are leveling up their skills as nonfiction writers.

We've chosen to use several masterworks—with the most considerable emphasis on *The Fire Next Time* by James Baldwin and *In Defense of Food* by Michael Pollan—as the maps to guide us throughout *What's the Big Idea?*

Although Baldwin and Pollan write on

different topics and in different styles over half a century apart, both men had an enormous cultural impact. They extended that influence to a broad popular audience with these works. We could have chosen many other titles, and we'll include examples from some others where it's helpful.

After reading this short, macro-principles primer, you may want to take a microscopic dive into Big Idea nonfiction by looking at *The Story Grid Masterwork Guide to Malcolm Gladwell's The Tipping Point,* which provides a scene-by-scene analysis of another exemplary title. We hope you'll be inspired to find your own favorite masterworks to learn from and apply Story Grid Methodology yourself. We'll provide some tips on how to do that too.

With Baldwin and Pollan as our touchstones, we've organized this book around a series of questions and answers that will explain how and why Big Idea books work.

1

HOW DO I KNOW IF I'M WRITING BIG IDEA NONFICTION?

First, put your "aha" to the Venn diagram test.

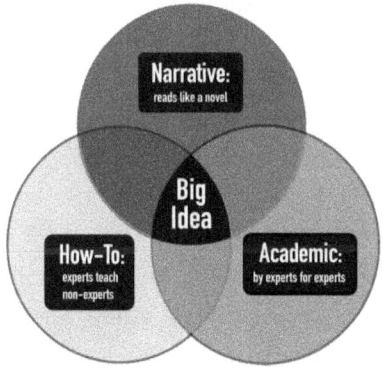

You've started your writing journey with a particular phenomenon or problem that fascinates you, and you just can't escape the urge to explore it. You've probably had an "aha" moment when you've recognized a new angle or insight about your topic. You've probably scratched out some notes, written a blog post, or even furiously drafted several chapters of something that needs a global structure to hold it all together. Now you realize you don't know exactly how to form that comprehensive organization.

What's the best form for this project? A structure that, in the most accessible way, will attract the broadest possible readership.

The first order of business is to decide whether the information and ideas you want to share should be in the form of *an academic work, a how-to, a narrative,* or *a Big Idea book*, which combines elements of the first three. This question may seem simple, but as editors, we've often found that it can take weeks, or even months, of writing and thinking before our clients understand their subjects and their ideal audience well enough to know the answer.

Part of the process of writing nonfiction is allowing the research to guide you to new places and new insights, so it's okay if you make changes in the structure of your book along the way. We've met many writers who begin writing a Big Idea book and end up with a narrative memoir or a how-to book—or vice versa. That's just part of the process. Don't lose heart if you're confused. Everyone gets confused.

Most nonfiction books, no matter which category they're in, have some sort of "aha" component—a new way of looking at a topic or question. But only in a Big Idea book does the writer structure the book so that it includes elements of academic, narrative, and how-to nonfiction built around a single central "aha" *revelation*.

Let's look at the characteristics of each of the four types of nonfiction so you can start to narrow the options for your book.

2

ACADEMIC NONFICTION

If you're a professor, a physician, or another kind of expert with highly specialized knowledge, chances are you know whether you're writing an academic book because you know your audience is made up of other experts in your field. That niche, but highly skilled, audience, will hold you—and you'll hold yourself—to a rigid standard of evidence and analysis, and you'll probably downplay your own author's voice. You'll follow standard guidelines within your community that determine the structure of your book.

Examples of academic nonfiction that have been highly influential on Story Grid Methodology include *Dynamics in Action: Intentional Behavior as a Complex System* by Alicia Juarrero and *Gödel, Escher, Bach: An Eternal Golden Braid* by Douglas Hofstadter. Both works assume their readers will have a working understanding of scientific fundamentals and a strong grasp of the humanities. They do not begin at first principles but rather assume the reader has a core knowledge within the realm of their inquiry.

But if you're an expert who wants to reach *a wider audience,* one that needs a logical progression of ideas from common sense on up, you'll have to adapt your work and approach to fit into the mold of narrative, how-to, or Big Idea nonfiction.

Most of us don't come in contact with much academic nonfiction—unless it makes a significant impact in the world—and even then, it's more likely that you'll hear about a critical academic book because of an article in a newspaper or magazine, rather than reading it firsthand. Hofstadter's book is the perfect example of an academic work that was so highly praised it sold extraordinarily well (and even does still today). But very few readers have actually made it from page one to the end. Other examples of breakthrough academic works include Alan Jasanoff's *The Biological Mind,* Annette Gordon-Reed's *The Hemingses of Monticello: An American Family,* and Thomas Kuhn's *The Structure of Scientific Revolutions.*

3

NARRATIVE NONFICTION

If you're a journalist, a memoirist, a historian, or just someone who has a compelling tale to share with a broad audience, the narrative format is tailor-made for you. The subjects you can explore are endless, as long as there are connected characters and events. Usually, there's some movement through time, but that doesn't mean the events must be told in chronological order. In narrative nonfiction, *the story is the star*. You'll use the tools and techniques of a fiction writer to tell a true story in a dramatic way that will grip readers' imaginations. You'll need to provide rich, specific details about the setting and cast of characters, and most importantly, a cathartic moment in the end, just like good novels have.

Memoir, history, and journalism focused on politics, natural science, and social science are among the most popular kinds of narrative nonfiction, and they dominate the lists of prize-winning books each year precisely because they captivate readers. Some examples of recent masterworks in this category include Tara Westover's *Educated* and Hope Jahren's *Lab Girl* (memoirs); Taylor Branch's *Parting the Waters* and Doris Kearns Goodwin's *No Ordinary Time* (histories); and David Quammen's *The Tangled Tree* and Rebecca Skloot's *The Immortal Life of Henrietta Lacks* (science journalism).

But if *analyzing a phenomenon or problem* is more important to you than telling a single compelling story, you'll need the structure of a Big Idea book instead of a narrative.

4
HOW-TO NONFICTION

Maybe you're an expert in gardening, time management, or child psychology who would like to share your knowledge, experience, and pro tips with the masses. Like academic nonfiction, how-to books target a specific audience that wants valuable information. But in this case, the experts translate their ideas into more straightforward language and careful, step-by-step instructions so ordinary people without degrees or special skills can make, understand, or survive something.

Nonfiction bestseller lists are full of how-to books, especially in the United States, because we have a cultural proclivity to want to improve ourselves and our situation in life. There are how-to books for every need. If you've been in a bookstore recently, you've seen James Clear's *Atomic Habits,* Tim Ferriss's *The 4-Hour Workweek,* Marie Kondo's *The Life-Changing*

Magic of Tidying Up, and Jen Sincero's *You Are a Badass: How to Stop Doubting Your Greatness and Start Living an Awesome Life,* to name just a few. Crafting a how-to book often can be an indispensable first step for authors to take before jumping into the deep end with a Big Idea.

So, how-to books provide step-by-step instructions to solve a complicated problem or multiple problems. Narrative nonfiction uses the fiction writer's toolbox to tell a story about historical or contemporary events. And, an academic work focuses on grand global theories that explain complex known data within a sizable phenomenal domain to people already engrossed by that domain. So, what's the Big Idea book?

5
BIG IDEAS + COGNITIVE SCIENCE

Big Idea books combine elements of each of the three types of nonfiction discussed above. The ultimate point of a Big Idea book is to help your readers think in a new way about a specific problem or phenomenon and to spread that new way of thinking to others. In the process, Big Idea titles teach readers how to cultivate knowledge and wisdom. Let's back up a little bit to get a sense from Shawn of how cognitive science can help us understand what it means to "cultivate knowledge:"

Contemporary "Four-E" Cognitive Science (a discipline that explores how our minds and bodies coordinate sense-making and behavior through embodied, embedded, enacted, and extended processes) operates under a **four flavors of knowledge model**, which evolved out of philosophy.

The first flavor is called **propositional**

knowledge, which is a statement of how to make something or a proposal about the way something works. It's an abstract mind transfer of information. Think of it as a direction someone offers you to solve a problem. The proposition only lives in your mind until...

You test the propositional knowledge procedurally. This process cultivates **procedural knowledge**, the second flavor. That is, you figure out if the proposition conforms to reality. In physics class, the teacher tells students that force equals the mass of an object multiplied by its acceleration, a Newtonian proposition. The next thing she does is an experiment to confirm that the proposition is true. The class witnesses the procedure of the test, measures the results, and compares them to the proposition. If the proposition works procedurally (F=ma), it's becoming truer or more real.

After procedural knowledge is confirmed, you'll want to test if the proposition works in multiple subjective contexts, or different perspectives. This process cultivates **perspectival knowledge**. That is, does the experiment work if you do it in a different laboratory? Does it work the same when it's a different day of the week? Does it work when the temperature outside is below zero? What about when it's summer? Does it work in multiple contexts across time and space? Does it work for your lab partner? What about in a science class in Ethiopia? Different perspectives that confirm the proposition increase the probability that the proposition aligns with reality—that it's true universally as opposed to just being true one time for one person in one place.

Lastly, there is **participatory knowledge**. This is the best test for across-the-board objective factual cause-and-effect knowledge. Participatory knowledge requires a community of people coming together to consider a proposition or propositions, and then all committing themselves to put the propositions into practice. These multiple perspectival contexts (each person tests the procedural component of the proposition in their particular environment) must then be brought together again. When the individuals of the group bring their multiple perspectival points of data back to the hive, the propositions can be analyzed again with an extraordinarily large amount of data. This new participatory knowledge can then be used to refresh and/or reformulate the propositions so that they conform as tightly as possible to reality.

This four-stage knowledge generation process is how The Story Grid Methodology evolves. Shawn Coyne created a whole series of propositions in his book, based upon his professional career, testing them procedurally and through his perspective as a fiction editor in book publishing. Then he invited our colleagues and us to come into the hive and add more participatory data to test his propositions in a whole slew of other arenas with a wide variety of constraints and conditions. We come together periodically to share our data and then revisit and refresh Shawn's propositions so they work in as large a context as possible. This very book evolved through that process as well.

Okay, let's see if we can link these four flavors of knowledge to our nonfiction categories. That is, if there are four types of knowledge, perhaps our four categories of nonfiction actually align and map onto these different ways of "knowing." Perhaps each kind of nonfiction contributes something indispensable to the global pursuit of knowledge. Knowing which category aligns with what kind of knowledge pursuit will be extremely useful when we inevitably get lost in the weeds of our writing. We can always step away and remind ourselves which kind of knowledge we're trying to elucidate.

Propositional knowledge is the substance of our **academic category** of nonfiction. These grand theories and ideas are generated among people who have dedicated their lives to the pursuit of integrating the unknown into our known world. They operate at the edge of the known and propose theories and hypotheses to be tested.

Procedural knowledge is the substance of our **how-to category** of nonfiction. These books are the practical experiments we can do that will teach us how to cause an effect. We follow the directions and practice the procedures, and voila, we get a particular result that generally aligns with our prediction.

Perspectival knowledge is the substance of our **narrative category** of nonfiction. Narrative is inherently subjective. We learn by looking at the world through the eyes of someone else, in this case often a historical figure or figures. We walk in their shoes to learn how another subjective human being came to navigate a pathway to a meaningful life. Or how they failed to.

Which brings us to **Participatory knowledge.**

Generating participatory knowledge is the substance of our **Big Idea category** of nonfiction. This integrating category takes individual propositions, procedures, and perspectives and extends them into groups.

So Big Idea books are, at their core, about teaching readers how to gain knowledge and cultivate wisdom. They offer a proposition. Then they tell an idiosyncratic story about how one can test a proposition, which requires accumulating data from multiple perspectives. Only by effectively showing this work can the Big Idea be taken seriously as expressing some element of the essential underlying truth of a particular phenomenon.

This three-part construction can magically transform into participatory exploration.

How's that?

The higher the number of people engaged by a Big Idea book, the more likely they are to find one another in the real world. And once they do, they end up discussing the propositions, procedures, and perspectives the author brought to bear and, in the process, they analyze and refresh the underlying truth of the idea. They participate in making the idea better.

It's extremely important to understand that Big Idea books, by definition, do not represent incontrovertible truth. There's very little of that to begin with, so critiquing a Big Idea book based upon whether or not it aligns perfectly with universal truth is a giant mistake. Rather Big Idea books represent a category that teaches us *how to pursue truth*. They may not provide certainty and will have flaws, but they artfully attune us by dissipating a lot of noise.

They define a clear realm of inquiry, which focuses our attention and allows us to consider the phenomenon with fresh frames of reference.

Cool, but how do you accomplish such an abstract thing?

6

BUILDING THE BIG IDEA

Use the research and analysis tools of academic nonfiction, add some fascinating stories and characters to grip readers' imaginations from narrative nonfiction, and finally offer some practical tools and step-by-step instructions so that readers can put the Big Idea into practice.

If that soup is tasty and compelling, the book measurably improves a reader's own life and, sometimes, by extension, the world for others around them. A well-executed Big Idea book teaches the reader how he or she or they can participate in cultivating wisdom for themselves, and more importantly, for everyone.

Let's get into some examples.

- When Shawn Coyne analyzed

Daniel Pink's *Drive,* he labeled it a Big Idea book. He supported that categorization by explaining that the author deeply researched the motivations behind people's pursuit of excellence in their work using the tools and approach of an academic. Pink then introduced stories and characters that engaged readers. Lastly, he then *formalized* a structural and functional organization about motivation, explaining a practical procedure for how to motivate employees, which is the meat of the middle of his book. He then invited the reader to take his ideas out for a test drive to see if they work.

- In *The Fire Next Time,* James Baldwin brought wisdom and analysis based on reading deeply in history, theology, and philosophy to the state of race relations in the 1960s. He drew portraits of unforgettable characters and events in his own life that provoked readers to anger and tears, and finally he suggested a radical form of love to help black and white Americans see each other differently and change each other's consciousness. He invited readers to try out his idea.

- Michael Pollan wrote *In Defense of Food* after *The Omnivore's Dilemma,* which explored the way our modern industrialized food system works. To answer the question readers of the earlier book posed—*What should we eat?*—Pollan wrote what he called an "eater's manifesto," overturning the conventional wisdom that nutritionists have all the answers. Pollan's defense rests on debunking nutrition science, tracing how our eating habits have changed over time, and shining a light on the food-industrial complex that drives modern food choices. The how-to of his manifesto was designed to make us healthier by trading "edible food-like substances" for real food. He invited us to participate in his idea.

Big Idea books start with a proposition that moves to analysis and formulation of a blueprint that is tested across multiple perspectives with an implied invitation to try it out yourself. Again, three flavors of knowledge are represented in Big Idea books, and those three encourage a fourth—the reader's participation in spreading the idea.

7
WHAT'S THE BIG IDEA OF A BIG IDEA BOOK?

Let's get back on the ground.

Your Big Idea is the answer to an inciting question, the question that set you off on the journey in the first place.

For example, Pollan's readers asked him: "How do we know what to eat to be healthy?" He wrote 250 pages and answered, "Eat food. Not too much. Mostly plants."[1]

When you read a Big Idea book, the way you think about a problem or a phenomenon in the world changes. Your mind expands a little, and you feel the power of a *revelation* that upends what you thought you already knew about your subject, the way Michael Pollan upended ideas about nutrition science.

As you're developing an outline for your book, ask yourself: *What new wisdom have I gained that I want to pass on to my readers?* And it will probably help to consider a few smaller questions leading up to the big one:

- Did you walk into your research with one way of looking at or solving a problem but leave thinking something different?
- Can you describe a revelatory moment you had while doing your research in one or two sentences?
- Can you create a flowchart or mind map to show some of the questions and answers that make up your research and describe the links among them?

Don't worry if you find it difficult to answer these questions at first, or if you change your answers a dozen or more times as you write. That's par for the course!

The Big Idea of your book will evolve.

The most important thing we tell clients is that you must keep returning to your inciting question and your Big Idea answer again and again as your word count grows. The macro lens discerns the micro field you'll need to develop in high-resolution.

If you'd like to see some examples of well-honed Big Ideas, you will find them in the first few pages (and often repeated in the last few pages) of almost all Big Idea books. Here are some examples:

- *In Defense of Food*: "Eat food. Not too much. Mostly plants."[2]
- *The Fire Next Time*: "You know, and I know, that the country is celebrating one hundred years of freedom one hundred years too soon. We [African Americans] cannot be free until they [white Americans] are free."[3]
- In *Daring Greatly,* Brené Brown says: "Vulnerability is not weakness... Our willingness to own and engage with our vulnerability determines the depth of our courage and the clarity of our purpose; the level to which we protect ourselves from being vulnerable is a measure of our fear and disconnection."[4]
- In *Silent Spring,* Rachel Carson says: "I do contend that we have put poisonous and biologically potent chemicals indiscriminately into the hands of persons largely or wholly ignorant of their potentials for harm...we have allowed these chemicals to be used with little or no advance investigation of their

effect on soil, water, wildlife, and man himself. Future generations are unlikely to condone our lack of prudent concern for the integrity of the natural world that supports all life."[5]

- And to go old school, in *On the Origin of Species,* Charles Darwin says, "As many more individuals of each species are born than can possibly survive; and as, consequently, there is a frequently recurring struggle for existence, it follows that any being, if it vary however slightly in any manner profitable to itself, under the complex and sometimes varying conditions of life, will have a better chance of surviving, and thus be naturally selected. From the strong principle of inheritance, any selected variety will tend to propagate its new and modified form."[6]

8

WHAT LIFE VALUE IS AT STAKE IN A BIG IDEA BOOK?

Big Idea nonfiction is fundamentally about *exploration and revelation*—the creation of new knowledge in the process of cultivating wisdom. You're moving readers along a continuum from *ignorance to wisdom,* and that movement is called a *life value shift.* It's one of the most important things to keep in mind as you write each scene.

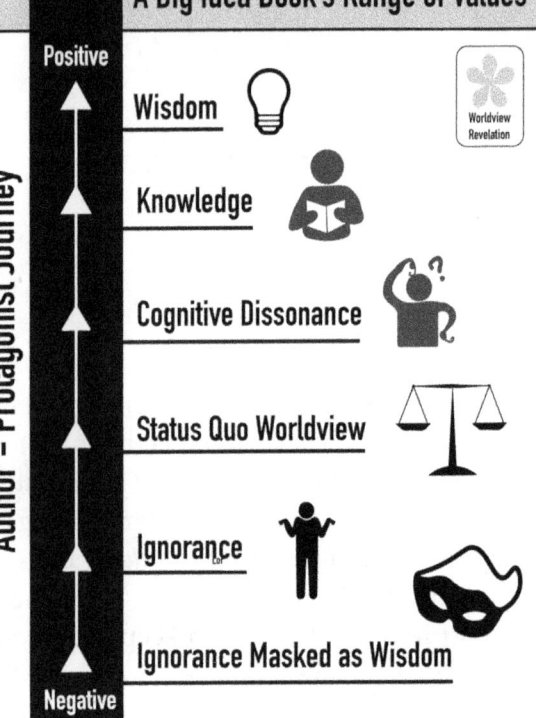

You'll need to take careful note of the critical life value shifts in each scene of your book because in both fiction and nonfiction, if your scenes do not embody a change in life value, readers will lose interest. Now, every single scene will not be on the ignorance-to-wisdom continuum—that would get pretty tedious, pretty fast. Sometimes scenes will focus on illustrative stories, and in those cases, the life values will shift along another continuum, such as death-to-life or injustice-to-justice, depending upon the story being told.

Let's look at how our masterworks handle life value shifts:

> • *In Defense of Food* has a passage that directly lands on the ignorance-to-wisdom spectrum, which includes cognitive dissonance (see graphic above). The life value changes in this passage from intense *cognitive dissonance* to *knowledge* and sets us up for the ultimate goal of *wisdom* in our food choices. It's clearly an essential step in answering the question that sent us on this journey in the first place: *What should we eat in order to be healthy?* And of course, because our health is at stake,

this is also moving us along the death-to-life value spectrum.

"[I]t turns out we don't need to declare our allegiance to any one of these schools of thought [the many conflicting and confusing claims of nutritionists] in order to figure out how best to eat. In the end, they are only theories, scientific explanations for an empirical phenomenon that is not itself in doubt: People eating a Western diet are prone to a complex of chronic diseases that seldom strike people eating more traditional diets. Scientists can argue all they want about the biological mechanisms behind this phenomenon, but whichever it is, the solution to the problem would appear to remain very much the same: *Stop eating a Western diet.*"[1]

• In *The Fire Next Time*, Baldwin has a critical scene in which the main life value changes from *being silenced* to *having a voice*, or a shift from young James repressing his feelings to expressing them openly, specifically in relation to his domineering father. But the story is also a building block in his movement from ignorance to wisdom, as he tries to understand how religion and race divide people:

"My best friend in high school was a Jew. He came to our house once, and afterward my father asked, as he asked about everyone, 'Is he a Christian?' — by which he meant 'Is he saved?'

I really do not know whether my answer came out of innocence or venom, but I said coldly, 'No. He's Jewish.'

My father slammed me across the face with his great palm, and in that moment everything flooded back—all the hatred and all the fear, and the depth of a merciless resolve to kill my father rather than allow my father to kill me—and I knew that all those sermons and tears and all that repentance and rejoicing had changed nothing. I wondered if I was expected to be glad that a friend of mine, or anyone, was to be tormented forever in Hell, and I also thought, suddenly, of all the Jews in another Christian nation, Germany. They were not so far from the fiery furnace after all, and my best friend might have been one of them.

I told my father, 'He's a better Christian than you are,' and walked out of the house. The battle between us was in the open, but that was all right; it was almost a relief. A more deadly struggle had begun."[2]

Big Idea Books gain in power the more willing the writer is to concretely commit to visceral life value shifts.

9

WHAT IS THE MACRO STRUCTURE OF A BIG IDEA BOOK?

If we look at Big Idea books from a macro, or thirty-thousand-foot, viewpoint we can see three clear steps in the intellectual adventure stories they tell: *analyzing, formalizing,* and *mechanizing.* These parts map to the beginning, middle, and end of every story.

Beginning Hook: This section of the book is all about *analyzing the phenomenon or problem* and finding intriguing patterns. In other words, you hook the reader by offering examples of the phenomenon or problem and asking, "Do you ever wonder why?" The beginning hook culminates in presenting the thesis explanation: "This happens because of A, B, and C," or "X, Y, and Z can solve this problem." The analysis hook usually accounts for the first ten percent or so of the Big Idea book.

Middle Build: This section, which is up to 80 percent of a Big Idea book, is where you *formalize* the analysis into a system that explains how the phenomenon or problem is structured and organized and how it functions. You use reason and specific examples. In other words, you take the phenomenon or problem apart and lay all of its pieces out on your intellectual lawn as if you're taking apart a bicycle to see how it works. Then, after consulting with experts and some published research, you slowly, rationally, put the thing back together to see if you've understood it—and if it still works.

Ending Payoff: In this final section of the book, you *mechanize* the explanation you've come up with so others can use it as a tool too. This takes up approximately the final 10 percent of the book. Here you're able to help readers see how they can understand the phenomenon or problem just like you did and use that knowledge to their benefit.

Armed with this understanding of the basic structure, let's look at how one of our authors does this.

Baldwin's Beginning Hook takes the form of a letter to his nephew, telling a personal story of his own father's life and prompting readers to wonder why it had to be so tragic. He suggests that his father "was defeated before he died because, at the bottom of his heart, he really believed what white people said about him."[1] But Baldwin then moves on to the broader thesis of the book, telling his nephew that "we, with love, shall force our [white] brothers to see themselves as they are."[2]

The **Middle Build** of *The Fire Next Time* includes firsthand memories of Baldwin's life, research into the history of imperialism in Africa, the Cold War, and contemporary (the 1960s) US politics. He takes apart the problem of racism and looks at it through many lenses, both micro and macro.

And in the **Ending Payoff**, Baldwin deepens his understanding of the problem of racism further, suggesting that not separatism and not violence, but love and connection between "the relatively conscious whites and the relatively conscious blacks" is a way of changing the world.[3]

10

HOW DO I SATISFY THE EXPECTATIONS OF THE BIG IDEA BOOK AUDIENCE?

Let's now take a look at the more specific "must-have" elements of Big Idea books, or what Shawn Coyne defines as their *Conventions and Obligatory Scenes,* and how you can use these to satisfy your readers' expectations while still surprising and engaging them at every turn. We'll include some examples from our masterworks, but you'll want to pick a work that resonates with you and analyze it for lessons that apply to the kind of book you want to write.

Remember: Your masterwork doesn't have to cover the same phenomenon, problem, or even the same broad subject as your own project. You're looking for a book in which the structure and approach inspire you to think creatively. Celebrated food writer Samin Nosrat says she struggled through four completely different drafts of her bestseller, *Salt, Fat, Acid,*

Heat before finding a work that spoke to her and helped her find the right approach. It wasn't a cookbook or a Michael Pollan food book. It was John McPhee's *Levels of the Game*, a book about a tennis match!

Conventions and Obligatory Scenes in Big Idea Nonfiction

If you're acquainted with The Story Grid's approach to fiction, you will know about the Conventions and Obligatory Scenes of fiction genres. If not, here's a quick review.

In a work of fiction: *Conventions* are the characters, settings, and means of turning the plot that set up reader expectations for the genre and *establish the global life value*. They create the conditions for a particular kind of change in a story—and we know stories are all about change.

Obligatory Scenes are events, revelations, and decisions that pay off reader expectations and *turn the global life value*. So, if Conventions set up the conditions for change, the Obligatory Scenes are the *causes* of a particular change in a story.

In nonfiction, Conventions and Obligatory Scenes operate in almost the same way as in fiction. In Big Idea Nonfiction:

Conventions are the ingredients that set up

the global life value change, which you'll remember is always on the spectrum of Ignorance to Knowledge to Wisdom.

Obligatory Scenes are the *Inquiry Events* that actually turn the global life value from Ignorance to Knowledge to Wisdom.

11

CONVENTIONS OF BIG IDEA NONFICTION

Cast of Characters

1. Author-protagonist: The author is the protagonist or hero in Big Idea books, and by extending a hand to us and taking us on a step-by-step journey of discovery, we readers are the protagonists and heroes too. Unlike academic authors, Big Idea authors often reveal quite a lot about themselves because we need to get to know the protagonist.

As an author-protagonist in all his books, Michael Pollan explores human relationships with the natural world, which includes plants and foods, and he takes us along with him. By relying on the authority of tradition and common sense, the source of advice on what to eat before the rise of experts, he invites us to do the same. Inspired by his childhood hero

George Plimpton, Pollan often inserts himself into stories as an amateur and an outsider, explaining, "That quality of wonder, of first sight, is available really only to the person doing something for the first time."[1]

In other words, if you're willing to do your research, don't be afraid of the role of the amateur observer when you write your Big Idea book.

2. *Sidekicks:* These characters exemplify particular components of the global hypothesis or idea, and they are crucial to the success of a Big Idea book. Your sidekicks will bring different perspectives to complicate and enrich your story. Michael Pollan explains his approach:

> "I don't believe any one perspective can unlock a subject ... Nonfiction gets interesting when you multiply the perspectives, or layer the different lenses that you bring to bear ... Each chapter is going to represent a different lens on the subject, and I'm going to circle it from these different points of view. And that, to me, is how you make nonfiction rich."[2]

In *The Fire Next Time*, Baldwin introduces

us to his nephew, his father, church leaders, Elijah Muhammad of the Nation of Islam, Malcolm X, and ordinary people—both black and white—he has met whose experiences informed his ideas.

Pollan also looks through many different lenses in writing *In Defense of Food,* illuminating the viewpoints of activists who were talking about our relationship with food a century ago including Dr. Weston Price, a dentist who traveled the world studying native cultures and the links between diet and physical and dental health, and Sir Albert Howard, a botanist and early proponent of organic agriculture who explored the relationships between healthy soil and healthy people, crops, and livestock.

3. Villain or Force of Antagonism: The villain or force of antagonism in a Big Idea book is the roadblock, or what stands in the way of understanding the phenomenon or solving the problem.

In most Big Idea books, the villain is abstract. So, for example, in Malcolm Gladwell's *The Tipping Point,* the force of antagonism is the human condition of ignorance and weakness; in Atul Gawande's *Being Mortal,* it is our modern fear and ignorance of death. For Baldwin, the foes are racism and hate, fueled by blindness to the humanity of others. For Pollan and Rachel Carson, the villains are a little more concrete: entrenched business interests and the scientists and government agencies that keep us using dangerous chemicals or eating what is produced in unhealthy food industries.

As an author, you should think about what specific foe you have to defeat to finish your journey toward wisdom.

Setting

The setting is the global arena in which the problem or phenomenon operates, usually a significant internal or external canvas.

Baldwin's large canvas is Western civilization corrupted by racism and hate, often zooming in for a close-up on the United States in the twentieth century. Pollan looks at modern Western industrialized nations, particularly the United States, where eating a typical modern diet causes people to suffer from preventable diseases, including obesity, heart disease, and diabetes. Brené Brown and James Clear are painting on the canvas of individuals' inner lives and mindsets.

Means of Turning the Plot

As we've already seen, a Big Idea usually defies conventional wisdom. You think a phenomenon is caused by X, but it's really caused by Y. Your Big Idea theory will be most intriguing to readers if it is counterintuitive.

In *The Tipping Point*, for example, Malcolm Gladwell let his audience in on a surprising theory: "Ideas and products and messages and behaviors spread just like viruses do."[3] Nearly two decades after Gladwell published his book, that statement seems obvious, but when he first shared it, this was a radically different way of thinking about rapid social change. His book overturned conventional wisdom, added a new term to our everyday vocabulary, and stayed on the bestseller lists for years.

Forms of Argument: Ethos, Logos, and Pathos

Every Big Idea book uses three classic forms of argument to persuade readers. The subject of your book will determine which type of persuasion you will use most frequently and effectively.

Ethos relies on the bona fides of the author and whether they are someone readers should trust. It elucidates the writer's propositional approach, how they came to propose the big idea. Do they have experience or expertise in the arena in which they are writing? Atul Gawande is a physician with the credibility and credentials to explain issues of life and death in *Being Mortal*. Rachel Carson's warning about an ecological crisis caused by pesticides in *Silent Spring* carried so much weight because of her years of fieldwork as a biologist.

However, many writers—especially journalists—take pride not in their expertise, but in their amateur status and ability to do the necessary research when they begin writing about a problem or phenomenon.

Logos depends on evidence, data, and all the experts and observers the author gathers to support their conclusions; it's aligned with procedural knowledge. Because Pollan comes to his subject as an amateur, he piles on the historical, scientific, and experiential research. When did food choice become difficult? When did Western diseases arise? He presents data to answer these questions and research showing that the majority of deaths in the United States are linked to diet.

Baldwin's evidence is primarily based on history and the experiences of people he knows well. For example:

"The treatment accorded the Negro during the Second World War marks, for me, a turning point in the Negro's relation to America...You must put yourself in the skin of a man who is wearing the uniform of his country, is a candidate for death in its defense, and who is called a 'n—' by his comrades-in-arms and his officers; who is almost always given the hardest, ugliest, most menial work to do; who knows that the white G.I. has informed the Europeans that he is subhuman...and who watches German prisoners of war being treated by Americans with more human dignity than he has ever received at their hands. And who, at the same time, as a human being, is far freer in a strange land than he has ever been at home."[4]

Pathos relies on an appeal to the emotions of the audience, arousing anger or tears or laughter. In this form of argument, the storytelling techniques of fiction are crucial to success. In this perspectival arena of knowledge generation, the hypothesis is tested.

When he begins a chapter packed with statistics and scientific studies about the contagious behaviors of teen suicide and smoking, Malcolm Gladwell lays aside ethos and logos for a few pages. He tells one of the most compelling stories in his book about a boy named Sima. The simple tale ends with a heartbreaking suicide note.[5] That story engages readers emotionally and carries them through the rest of the chapters, searching for answers.

Multiple Points of View

And what about the narrative device, or in other words, who is telling the story? Because of the personal revelations involved in Big Idea books, the point of view is often a narrator based on the author's persona. Still, the points of view and voices of sidekick experts are usually well represented too. Gladwell uses the same narrative device in almost every book, article, speech, and podcast episode—and it has become his trademark. In Shawn Coyne's words, Gladwell's narrative device is "a nerd who likes to figure things out."[6]

Different points of view require different tones. When Pollan presents scientific evidence, he writes with a healthy dose of skepticism, but overall, his tone is often irreverent, and he enjoys challenging sacred cows. Remember, you don't have to give your sources a pass just because they have PhDs; you can question them!

Third-person omniscient (the most authoritative point of view), first-person omniscient, first-person plural, and second-person singular are all useful tools in a Big Idea book. For more information on point of view in nonfiction, see Shawn Coyne's article, "Four Nonfiction Points of View."[7] If you're trying to engage readers in a lively conversation with your ideas, the second person is especially valuable. Have you noticed how often we're using it here?

Narrative Cliffhangers

In addition to employing pathos in their arguments, nonfiction authors must make use of other novelists' tools that create narrative drive (mystery, suspense, and dramatic irony). Without narrative drive, a Big Idea Book won't hold the readers' interest, and they'll never reach the Big Reveal at the end. Big Idea writers keep us glued to the page by regulating the amount of information they provide—not too much and not too little.

In *The Fire Next Time*, one of the most extended passages is a dinner meeting between Baldwin and Nation of Islam leader Elijah

Muhammad in which readers wonder whether either man will persuade the other to his cause or whether a full-on battle will break out at any moment.

Set Pieces or Sequences

Mini stories within the global Big Idea story include a dilemma that must be solved before the global story can move forward. This is part of the process of unpacking the phenomenon or problem. Often, writers need to build sequences of stories to lead readers toward their more complex conclusions.

Pollan has to show step-by-step what caused people to abandon common sense and tradition at the dinner table in favor of scientific experts. So he uses a series of scenes to demonstrate a pattern:

1. At the end of the nineteenth century, nutritionists started thinking about food in terms of its identifiable constituent nutrients, which led to scientifically endorsed products and guidelines for health.
2. The new emphasis on invisible nutrients, as opposed to visible food, caused people to value

quantifiable nutrients over the quality of the whole food.
3. Food manufacturers embraced this approach, marketing processed products that were purported to be better than real, whole foods, using claims consistent with government guidelines.
4. Manufacturers changed with the times and stayed in sync with the latest scientific studies.[8]

This sequence establishes how and why people gave up common sense for scientific evidence and sets up another sequence showing that following nutritionists' and government advice failed to make people healthier.

External Genre Conventions

The main story in a Big Idea book is an internal one, tracking the author-protagonist's internal journey to knowledge, but there is also an external story. This story traces the forces (individual people, society, the environment) that create conflicts for the author-protagonist.

You'll find information about the nine external content genres at https://storygrid. com/what-we-talk-about-when-we-talk-about-genre/. These external genres include Action, Horror, Mystery, Western, Thriller, War, Society, Love, and Performance.

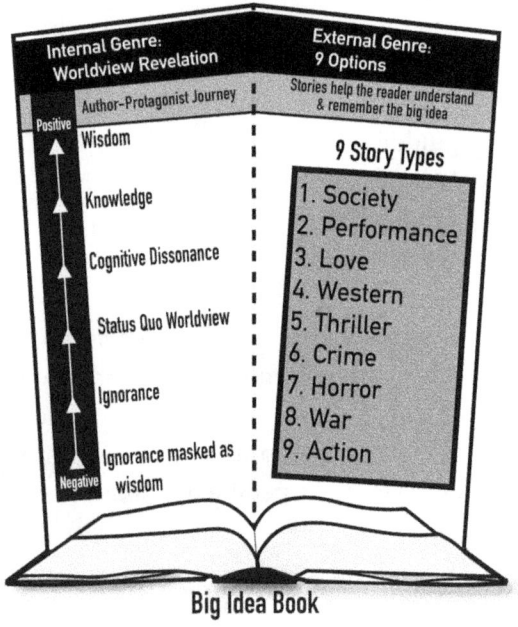

Big Idea Book

The Fire Next Time has an embedded external Society story, or more specifically, a Society-Historical story about racism in the United States and the Western world. Like all Society stories, it's about a shift in power—a revolution—with an enormous divide between those who have power and those who are disenfranchised.

In Defense of Food is an Action-Adventure-Labyrinth story, with life and death stakes. The villain (the food-industrial complex) uses a labyrinth (confusion about what to eat) against the victims (eaters) and hero (Pollan himself).

12

OBLIGATORY SCENES OF BIG IDEA NONFICTION

1. Establish the Problem or Phenomenon

The author-protagonist introduces the reader to the problem or phenomenon they will explore. In *The Tipping Point*, Gladwell introduces us to the phenomenon of dramatic, rapid, and unexplained change through two very different examples from the 1990s: Hush Puppies shoes, a brand that was dying before it suddenly went viral; and New York City's crime statistics, which tipped for the better.

2. Make a Clear Statement of the Big Idea

As we've discussed already, you must present your Big Idea and the arguments that support it in the Beginning Hook. The Big Idea is your hook. Don't withhold the hook!

3. Provide Evidence That Supports the Big Idea

Academic research, experiments, studies, and analysis are often key foundational evidence in a Big Idea book, as are interviews with experts in the field. We talk about the variety of types of evidence in the section on The Middle Build above.

In the Middle Build of *In Defense of Food,* Pollan explains how the rise of Nutritionism and the industrialization of agriculture, food processing, and eating led to our current unhealthy situation. Because people are so used to relying on experts, Pollan must show what's wrong with the approach of Nutritionism's proponents and how the industrialization of food has damaged our health. He uses academic research and experts in history and science to build his analysis.

4. Tell Entertaining or Compelling Anecdotes

Scenes that are funny, shocking, touching, or otherwise entertaining have become obligatory in modern Big Idea books. They're fodder for great conversations with friends, coworkers, and family. Gladwell made his name as a master of the juicy anecdote—a talent he recently turned into a new career as a podcast host. In *The Tipping Point,* for example, he tells us in great detail how the creators of *Blue's Clues* built on the success of *Sesame Street* to make learning even *"stickier"*. He brings the characters in each anecdote to life in just a few paragraphs—from Mark Alpert and his genius for choosing hotels and cars to a Chinese teacher mistaken for a spy. Every memorable story you share helps readers later recall and discuss your Big Idea, creating the participatory knowledge discussed in chapter 5.

Pollan, on the other hand, relies on a journalistic writing style that is less conversational than Gladwell's. Because of the nature of the problem he's unpacking, Pollan presents stories that are more compelling than entertaining, but they are just as memorable as Gladwell's. It's shocking to see how the villains of *In Defense of Food* manipulate facts and people to improve profit margins and how government agencies are complicit.

5. Give Some How-To Advice

Every Big Idea book includes some prescriptive information so readers will know how to apply the knowledge they've gained. In *Rising Strong: The Reckoning. The Rumble. The Revolution.*,

Brené Brown shows readers that to rise after falling, you must work with the stories you tell yourself when you're struggling. She explains step-by-step: first, you have a *reckoning*, in which you notice your emotional reactions and get curious about them; second, you *rumble* with those emotions by uncovering the stories you're telling about your struggles and interrogating them; and finally, you experience a *revolution* by applying what you learned and incorporating it into a daily practice.[1] The final how-to of Brown's book walks readers through how to apply each of these steps at work, at home, and in their communities.[2]

6. Present a Big Reveal

As a story with a narrative component, Big Idea nonfiction has a core event. The core event in a Big Idea book is when you reveal a *twist* or *more profound understanding* of the phenomenon or problem, convincing readers that what they've believed in the past is all wrong. It doesn't have to be shocking, like the twist in a horror movie, just something that moves your original idea to a more profound or counterintuitive level.

- In *The Tipping Point,* the revelation is a warning about the destructive power of tipping points. Gladwell suggests that although *"tipping"* a product, behavior, or idea from obscurity to ubiquity *can* be a positive phenomenon (for example, the rise of Hush Puppies and decline of New York crime), it also has a dark side (for example, the epidemic of teen suicide in Micronesia).

- In *Being Mortal*, physician Atul Gawande advocates that medical professionals deal with the end of life differently to improve the experience of death for patients. He reveals at the conclusion that the benefits of his approach are not just for patients but for their loved ones as well. In changing the way he helped his own father experience death, Gawande's life was enriched, and he and his family were able to experience greater peace.[3]
- In *We Should All Be Feminists,* Chimamanda Ngozi Adichie analyzes the problem of gender discrimination in her Nigerian homeland, advocating that Nigerian women embrace and remake the label of "feminist." In the final

pages, she reveals that the "best feminist" she knows is her brother Kene, and she wants to redefine the term so it applies to men and women. "My own definition of a feminist is a man or a woman who says, yes, there's a problem with gender as it is today and we must fix it, we must do better. All of us, women and men, must do better."[4]

- Gretchen Rubin created new knowledge about human personality in *The Four Tendencies*. Most of the book lays out the specifics of each "tendency" and its implications in practical daily life and interactions with other people. At the end of the book, Rubin reveals that someone at one of her public lectures provided her with the deeper meaning of her work by asking whether there are implications for overall happiness and success. "The happiest and most successful people," she says, "are those who have figured out how to exploit their tendency to their benefit, and just as important, how to counterbalance its limitations."[5] And she goes on to

offer how-to advice for achieving that balance.
- In the Big Reveal of *The Fire Next Time,* Baldwin helps readers see that not only does American society need a revolution in race relations but so does the entire world. To free humans from the bondage of false ideas about race, blacks and whites must connect "like lovers" and change each other, from the highest political and cultural realms to the most intimate personal realm.
- In *In Defense of Food,* Pollan explains that "The human animal is adapted to a wide range of different diets, but the Western diet, however you define it, does not seem to be one of them."[6] The good news of Pollan's reveal is that you don't have to figure out which scientists are correct. You just need to abandon the Western diet and hone your common sense with an eye toward how traditional cultures eat—through a more direct relationship with food.

13

HOW TO BUILD SCENES IN BIG IDEA NONFICTION

To define a scene in a work of fiction, you usually begin by asking yourself what the characters are *doing*, what they *want*, and how they *change*. In fiction, each scene is about conflict and change, even if the change is minor or only happens in the mind of one of the characters.

When you look at how individual scenes work in Big Idea books (or when writing your own), you'll often be tempted to focus on the details of the compelling stories because they feature the kinds of conflict and change with which we're familiar. To bring yourself back to the big picture, look at Inquiry Events.

Inquiry Events

A working scene in a Big Idea book contains at least one *Inquiry Event,* which is an *active change of life value* along the Ignorance to Knowledge to Wisdom spectrum in the author-protagonist. It's focused on the author's investigation of a particular question and can sometimes be hard to pinpoint.

The way to identify an **Inquiry Event** is to answer four questions:

1. What is the author-protagonist literally doing in the scene? What is the author-protagonist trying to do, show, or communicate about the Big Idea mentioned in the Beginning Hook or Introduction?

2. What is the author trying to accomplish in the scene? Why is the author-protagonist discussing this particular evidence (a story or some data) here and now?

3. What has changed along the Ignorance to Knowledge to Wisdom spectrum in the scene? You might go from having no questions to having many questions, for example.

4. What is the resulting Inquiry Event?

By answering these questions, you'll

usually be able to get to the heart of what's really happening in the scene.

The Five Commandments of Storytelling

In Big Idea nonfiction, the building blocks of your argument are *questions and answers* that build toward wisdom. So, the Five Commandments of each scene revolve around questions and answers:

> 1. **Inciting Incident:** You present a story, event, or fact about a particular phenomenon that gives rise to a question.

> 2. **Progressive Complications:** You present the results of your investigation of the question in the form of research or stories. These results push you closer to or further away from figuring out a component of the answer to the inquiry.

> **Until you reach a Turning Point Progressive Complication:** You find new evidence that sparks a revelatory insight that gives rise to a question.

> 3. **Crisis:** You face a dilemma about how

to apply the insight to the larger phenomenon or problem.

4. Climax: You resolve the Crisis by connecting the insight to the broader investigation.

5. Resolution: You present the Resolution as a convincing recap of the evidence collected to answer the question raised by the inciting incident and how you figured out how to integrate the insight into your overall Big Idea.

This is a brief introduction to how scenes work in Big Idea books. For a full analysis of how scenes work in a Masterwork, check out *The Story Grid Masterwork Guide to Malcolm Gladwell's The Tipping Point*.

14

HOW TO FIGURE OUT WHAT KIND OF NONFICTION BEST SERVES YOUR IDEA

Now that you understand what goes into a Big Idea book, you can decide whether it has the right combination of purpose, content, structure, and audience for your idea. Try answering these questions to home in on a decision:

Do you want to deliver detailed information to a small audience of experts and students in your field of expertise?

If so, write a work of academic nonfiction.

Do you want to reach a wider audience and adapt your ideas to include stories, narrative drive, and also provide how-to advice?

If so, write a Big Idea book.

Do you want to focus your writer's energy on telling a compelling, character-rich story to entertain and inform?

Write a piece of narrative nonfiction, which could take the form of a long article or book, whether it's a memoir, history, or journalism.

Or is the idea or problem you want to investigate more important than a single story?

If so, write a Big Idea book.

Do you want to help fix a problem for your readers, providing clear, step-by-step advice?

If so, write a how-to book.

Or do you need to help your readers think differently about a problem or phenomenon before they can effectively apply your how-to advice?

If so, write a Big idea book.

Finally, although it's a tricky proposition, if you are torn between two options, you could try to walk a high-wire and write a hybrid that includes elements of two types of nonfiction. In this case, you will benefit from searching for examples to guide you and talking it through with an editor to make sure you've chosen a path that will work.

15

ARE YOU READY TO SHOW UP? ARE YOU READY TO MAKE MISTAKES?

If you've gotten this far, it's now time to decide on the type of book you're going to write and begin. Yes, take our word for it, you may well change your mind after ten thousand words. And you are going to make mistakes. As Big Idea author Brené Brown says, "[I]f you're not failing, you're not really showing up!"[1]

Malcolm Gladwell, Michael Pollan, James Baldwin, Rachel Carson, and every other author we've mentioned all have armies of critics who dispute their sources, their analysis, and their conclusions. We think one of the most valuable lessons you can draw from studying any real master of Big Idea nonfiction is how important it is to acknowledge and even celebrate your own imperfection.

Remember this from chapter five?

It's extremely important to understand that Big Idea books, by definition, do not represent incontrovertible truth. There's very little of that to begin with, so critiquing a Big Idea book based upon whether or not it aligns perfectly with universal truth is a giant mistake. Rather Big Idea books represent a category that teaches us *how to pursue truth*. They may not provide certainty and will have flaws, but they artfully attune us by dissipating a lot of noise. They define a clear realm of inquiry, which focuses our attention and allows us to consider the phenomenon with fresh frames of reference.

Malcolm Gladwell's work is an excellent case in point. He makes mistakes, changes his mind, finds new evidence, and continues to question his ideas in book after book, article after article, podcast after podcast! As he said in an interview about his process:

> "I like discovering things. What happens is, I keep going back and discovering that what I thought five years ago isn't right. It's incomplete. The

idea that part of what it means to be human in the world and a thinking person is to constantly be correcting your beliefs is, to me, fascinating and addictive...It makes thinking an adventure."[2]

16

RESOLUTION

OUR SURPRISING BUT INEVITABLE CONCLUSION (WITH A TWIST)

> "Writers are great lovers. They fall in love with other writers. That's how they learn to write. They take on a writer, read everything by him or her, read it over again until they understand how the writer moves, pauses, and sees. That's what being a lover is: stepping out of yourself, stepping into someone else's skin."
>
> — Natalie Goldberg, *Writing Down the Bones: Freeing the Writer Within*[1]

At last! The Resolution of our journey through the wonderful world of nonfiction brings us to the moment when you really start working on your own book.

If you've had your *aha* or *Eureka* moment and read through this guide, but still feel unsure about what a good book looks like, our probably unsurprising and inevitable conclusion is that you should *keep reading* works that inform and inspire you. Choose a masterwork that resonates with you, whether because of the topic or the structure or the author's voice or any other reason. Analyze it deeply on your own.

To find great books, you can check out lists of prize-winning books from current and past years. The Pulitzers, National Book Awards, and local or niche-specific awards in science, politics, history, and other topics will yield well-crafted and intriguing options. Also, try combing interviews with authors you admire to find out what books have influenced them. And of course, ask friends and colleagues for their favorites. Let yourself get lost in the proliferation of year-end "best of" lists or websites that specialize in book recommendation, including FiveBooks.com and BookRiot.com.

Keep exploring! Chances are, you're going to have to read a lot of books to find the right mentors. The great news is, you'll be expanding your mind and thinking about the world in new ways as you seek those mentors.

If you'd like an in-depth look at one Big Idea book, Story Grid has published our *Story*

Grid Masterwork Guide to Malcolm Gladwell's The Tipping Point.

Now get out some three-by-five index cards, a spreadsheet, a cork-board, a Scrivener file, or whatever tools help you record, collate, shuffle, and make connections. Start researching and writing.

Remember that your favorite writers started just like you, with a few ideas and a blank page—struggling, failing, revising, and struggling some more.

Pack this guide and lunch (Eat food. Not too much...) and set out on your journey. Good luck!

ABOUT THE AUTHORS

LESLIE WATTS is a Story Grid Certified Editor, writer, and podcaster based in Austin, Texas. She's been writing for as long as she can remember—from her sixth-grade magazine about cats to writing practice while drafting opinions for an appellate court judge. As an editor, Leslie helps fiction and nonfiction clients write epic stories that matter. She believes writers become better storytellers through study and practice and that editors owe a duty of care to help writers with specific and supportive guidance. You can find her online at Writership.com.

SHELLEY SPERRY is a Story Grid Certified Editor, writer, and researcher based in Alexandria, Virginia. She used to work at National Geographic, so she thinks every book is better if it has a cool map, a dramatic landscape, or a lot of penguins. As a writer and researcher, Shelley works with nonprofit and business clients on environmental, labor, and education topics. As an editor, she specializes in nonfiction, helping authors tell true stories about the world. She agrees with Barbara Kingsolver, that "revision is where fine art begins." You can find her online at SperryEditorial.com.

NOTES

Introduction

1. William K. Zinsser, *On Writing Well,* 7th ed. (New York: HarperCollins, 2006), 34.

7. WHAT'S THE BIG IDEA OF A BIG IDEA BOOK?

1. Michael Pollan, *In Defense of Food: An Eater's Manifesto* (New York: Penguin, 2008), 1.
2. Ibid.
3. James Baldwin, *The Fire Next Time* (New York: Vintage International, 1993), 10.
4. Brené Brown, *Daring Greatly: How the Courage to Be Vulnerable Transforms the Way We Live, Love, Parent, and Lead* (New York: Avery, 2012), 2.
5. Rachel Carson, *Silent Spring,* 40th anniversary ed. (Boston: Mariner, 2002), 12-13.
6. Charles Darwin, *On the Origin of Species by Means of Natural Selection*, ed. Joseph Carroll (Peterborough, Canada: Broadview, 2003), 97.

8. WHAT LIFE VALUE IS AT STAKE IN A BIG IDEA BOOK?

1. Pollan, *In Defense of Food*, 140 (emphasis original).
2. Baldwin, 37.

9. WHAT IS THE MACRO STRUCTURE OF A BIG IDEA BOOK?

1. Baldwin, 4.
2. Baldwin, 10.
3. Baldwin, 105.

11. CONVENTIONS OF BIG IDEA NONFICTION

1. "Writing the Ineffable: Michael Pollan in Conversation with Elaine Scarry," YouTube video, 1:17:36, posted by Harvard University, January 9, 2019, https://youtu.be/cjbUnsuAs8o
2. "Michael Pollan on Writing: What Illuminates a Story?" YouTube video, 8:28, posted by Big Think, November 2, 2019, https://youtu.be/m2VXyBOmK3Q
3. Malcolm Gladwell, *The Tipping Point: How Little Things Can Make a Big Difference* (New York: Little, Brown, 2000), 7.
4. Baldwin, 49.
5. Gladwell, 216-217.
6. Shawn Coyne (Storygridding Nonfiction), interview with Tim Grahl, *Story Grid Podcast*, podcast audio, January 27, 2016, https://storygrid.com/storygridding-nonfiction/.
7. Shawn Coyne, "Four Nonfiction Points of View," *Story Grid* (blog), undated, https://storygrid.com/four-nonfiction-points-of-view/.
8. Pollan, 19-26, 27-31, 32-36, 37-40.

12. OBLIGATORY SCENES OF BIG IDEA NONFICTION

1. Brené Brown, *Rising Strong: The Reckoning. The Rumble. The Revolution.* (New York: Spiegel & Gau, 2015), 40-41.

2. Ibid., 256-267.
3. Atul Gawande, *Being Mortal: Medicine and What Matters in the End* (New York: Metropolitan Books, 2014).
4. Chimamanda Ngozi Adichie, *We Should All Be Feminists* (Anchor Books, 2015), 48.
5. Gretchen Rubin, *The Four Tendencies: The Indispensable Personality Profiles That Reveal How to Make Your Life Better (and Other People's Lives Better Too)* (New York: Harmony, 2017), 244.
6. Pollan, *In Defense of Food,* 100.

15. ARE YOU READY TO SHOW UP? ARE YOU READY TO MAKE MISTAKES?

1. "Brené Brown: Why Your Critics Aren't the Ones Who Count," YouTube Video, 17:18, posted by 99U, December 4, 2013, https://www.youtube.com/watch?v=8-JXOnFOXQk
2. "Malcolm Gladwell on Truth, Trump's Tweets, and Talking to Strangers," YouTube video, 44:18, posted by Channel 4 News, September 4, 2019, https://youtu.be/on7Wjdl_qhM

16. RESOLUTION

1. Natalie Goldberg, *Writing Down the Bones: Freeing the Writer Within* (Boston: Shambala, 2015), 86.

www.ingramcontent.com/pod-product-compliance
Lightning Source LLC
Chambersburg PA
CBHW051033030426
42336CB00015B/2857